IN HIS PRESENCE

EVA BELL WERBER

DEVORSS *Publications*

Seventh Printing, 1992

ISBN: 0-87516-102-2

DeVorss & Company, Publisher
P.O. Box 550
Marina del Rey, CA 90294

Printed in the United States of America

FOREWORD

To you who read with the heart, these
words shall be as a lighted lantern hung
by the roadside on a dark night. They
shall make light the way and easy the
path for you who journey.

CONTENTS

In His Presence

QUIETLY COMES MY BLESSING

As THE HEART is emptied of self you shall receive My blessing. It comes not with a loud trumpet call nor with the clang of bells, but with a mere whisper like the flutter of a bird's wing. Like the perfume of a rose wafted toward you, does My blessing fall.

Then shall it be manifested in many ways, in friends and in loved ones, in the guided pathway, as wishes deep from the heart are granted. It is so simple an act, just to be still and hold open the heart, then to go again about your work. So truly shall the blessings come and so full shall the harvest be, that you shall give all the room of your heart to receive its joy. You shall pour out again and yet again this service and blessing. Light shall be around and about you. Wait now, expecting to receive, for you have planted the seed and the harvest of good shall truly follow.

7

I WILL SPEAK TO YOU

I WILL SPEAK to you through the pages of this book words that shall sing for you down the years, words which shall tell of My great love and abiding presence. They will tell of My great rebuilding power in the human life, and how I so tenderly care for and direct Mine own. I will tell you of a world of beauty which is there for all to find, not a war-torn world, a world blasted apart by hate and selfishness, but a world of peace and love. You say, "Where can we now find such a world? Even after the shriek of bomb and shell is hushed, there is still desolation, misery, fear and despair. Shall there ever be a place where men hate and destroy not?"

Listen, My Beloved, and be at peace. You first must find this place you desire within your own heart. There in the garden of your soul you shall meet Me, your Beloved. My hand is laid in tenderness on your head. At its mystical touch the outer realm with its destruction, its confusion of purpose falls away. A great stillness shall pervade you and you shall only be conscious of the sweetness of the Holy Presence.

Then shall you be indeed in a world of peace, even as a world set aside, where conflicts cease and burdens fall away. Learn to pause often for My heavenly touch which carries such healing for the soul and from which all bodily healing and peace shall follow. So open your heart as you read these My words and take them unto yourself, for they are meant for you and whosoever will come to the fountain of My love.

YOUR FIRST LESSON

YOUR FIRST LESSON is to learn to be still for I can only speak to a hushed soul. When you can drop from your consciousness all outer clamor, then can My voice speak to you, teaching things of the soul which you needs must know for the soul's development. PRACTICE SILENCE AT ALL OPPORTUNITY. I shall then be enabled to come close to you. More and more shall it be made easy for you until in a moment's turning, at any time or in any place you can be alone with Me. You can feel the touch of My hand and know that My guidance and love are surrounding you. So shall you walk in peace. Joy shall crown every moment of your waking day and the night shall be filled with the glory of My Holy Presence.

☆   ☆   ☆

Make of your own house a house of peace and all the world shall be peace about you.

A LOVE SONG

MY VERY BELOVED, I would write for you a love song of the heart, I who am so close to you and who functions so completely within your physical body. I am as the perfume of all flowers within you. I release My perfume as from an alabaster box that it may delight your days, that it may fill the very air about you with a mystical sweetness, and all you contact shall be calmed and refreshed though they know not why. Yea, I am as a sweet perfume within you.

I am like sweet music. All sound is created by Me, and my creative work is fulfilled through you, My living harp. I play upon you and as with swift fingers I bring forth harmonies, for I am harmony within you.

O My Beloved, lend your ear not to discord, but tune it to Me. Know the Lover of your soul, and all that is complete in that love shall be yours. Give forth my love to all you contact for it is undiminishable, and as you give forth I shall be able to release more of My great abundance for your blessing.

ONLY FOR THIS MOMENT

ONLY FOR TODAY need you try to keep close our contact. Only for the present moment are you held responsible. Tomorrow, yea, even the next hour is yet unborn. So you see, after all, the task is not such a hard one. Hold fast to My hand now, this very moment feel its tender touch and verily you shall not be left alone in the next hour, day or month.

If you could but learn this lesson in its completeness, how full of joy would be your day. You fear that as you brush with the world about you, you will lose the sweetness of My presence. At that very instant the thought of the loss is separating us. Waste not time, thus. When that thought and fear comes gives thanks that at that very moment you can know Me, close and loving within your heart, and I say to you that it shall be a time of strength which shall never leave you.

Put this into practice and see with what sureness you walk your way. The consciousness of My Presence shall come to be ever with you, guiding and protecting you and strengthening you for any tasks that fall to your lot.

THE SPRING ZEPHYR

As GENTLE as a spring zephyr is My Presence felt in your heart. Learn to heed its faintest murmur. Feel My great divine inflow filling and flooding you and truly your strength shall never fail. Wherever you are, there am I, alive and vibrant in your consciousness.

As sweetheart of your soul do I caress you and flood your being with a glory of perfect love. You feel it a duty to love and worship Me, but I would have you love Me for love's sake alone. See Me in all things lovely. Feel the gentle touch of My hand as the breeze kisses your cheek.

As you meet Me in quiet meditation you shall go forth love filled and light filled. Again I say, not as a duty shall you love Me, but as the Beloved of your soul shall you give Me your love and adoration. Then and then only are you fitted to go forth in My service.

BEAUTY OF THE INNER REALM

Beloved, that which is beautiful in the outer realm is but an expression of the beauty within. Recognize all beauty as of Me when you see the loveliness with which I surround you in the realm of the material. May the beauty of tree and forest, fragrance of flowers and garden, glow of the starry night and shine of sunlit meadows always take you back with a thought of love and reverence to the One from whom all beauty emanates.

I would that you might have an ever growing consciousness of Me, and beauty shall crown your days. Share all that is lovely with others, but

never fail to share with them that which is real
and eternal.

☆   ☆   ☆

*I shall rise up within the vessel of My
expression and glorify Myself with abundant life, freedom and vitality. I shall
throw off the grave clothes with which
man would bind Me and rise triumphant
from the couch of pain, for I am Life and
abundant fullness of all things beautiful.
I am all there is.*

SEEK

SEEK AND YOU shall find. How can you have more
of My Presence in your consciousness unless you
come seeking it? The sun is warm upon your face,
yet if you draw the curtain, there is a chill in place
of the warm glow.

So it is, My dear one. I am warm as the
warmth of many suns within you, yet do you feel
Me not, for so long have you drawn the curtains of
sense consciousness between us. Let it not be so.
Rend the veils that hide Me from your keen enjoy-
ment. Only you can do this. You say that circumstances keep you in a sense of earth vibration.
When you feel it is hard to know the Holy Presence, I say it need not be so. Only as you make the
effort to shut out the earth noise and confusion, and

acknowledge My Presence and warmth within you, only as you bless and give thanks for that Presence, can a more complete consciousness of it be made manifest to you.

This is your lesson for today. Let us be still, reveling in the truth that I am close within and about you and all that touches your life shall wear the mark of Me and of being My choice for you.

TO HIM THAT ABIDETH

"HE THAT ABIDETH", not she who occasionally comes to the throne room of His heart, but to the one who abides there is the promise given. It is possible to so abide in quietness that even amid the great confusion of the day your whole being shall be permeated with a great calm and peace, and healing shall flow from you.

Only by thus abiding shall you be able to attain this high point of consciousness which I would have for you. Each morning as you feel the touch of My hand, in the silence as it is laid so gently on your head, you are blessed and carry the reflection of the Holy Presence all the busy day. Then do you partake of My virtues and share the attendant blessings. Pause now for My blessing on you and those you love and go forth to serve with joy and gladness of heart.

☆　　☆　　☆

All that I ask is a stilled mind in order that I may reflect My perfect likeness upon its surface.

THE JEWEL BOX OF LIFE

THE JEWEL BOX of life has a secret spring which when touched will open for you the beautiful jewels of love. Love is the key and love the spring and it will bring these fruits into manifestation. Learn to use this key daily and I promise you rich reward.

There is so much of hate expressed all about you and it brings only destruction to those who function by its expression. When you live by the rule of love all life is beautiful. As you give forth love it shall return again to enrich you. So remember, My child, that your life will be as a box of jewels and when you learn to use the key these jewels will be made available for your use.

☆　　☆　　☆

Go forth in My consciousness this day. Go forth as a ray of golden light and carry My blessing to all you meet.

THE HIDDEN SPRING

FEAR NOT! Allow Me to direct the path on which you journey. You cannot see nor can you know My

plan for you at this time. Know that I, the Beloved, hold all things in My hand and My plan
for you shall be revealed as I see fit. Let Me carry
the thing you fear, and know that back of it all is
My high purpose for your life. I have planned it
so and if you walk with Me you need not fear that
you shall lose the way of My direction.

So waste not precious time and energy in fear
and foreboding. Come often to the secret shrine
within your heart and I shall refresh you as from
a hidden spring of cool water and you shall again
step forth on the path, with lightened foot-steps
and a mind that is calm and fearless.

☆   ☆   ☆

*Let peace be in your heart and though
tumult roars about you, there can you
always retreat and find security.*

PEACE WITHIN

WHEN A PROBLEM confronts you that is seemingly
insurmountable, then is the time to turn quietly
within. Talk it over with the Beloved of your soul
to whom there are no problems and who knows in
its completeness the path you journey. Then shall
quiet peace come to you in place of disturbance.
There shall be a quiet waiting, as the quiet of the
dawn awaits the brilliant sunrise and ere you realize it I shall have taken care of that which so

troubles your heart. You will be shown your way and there will no longer be a problem to disturb you.

Rest in the knowledge that I who live and function through you, I Life Supreme, shall solve all your difficulties if you will but give them into My keeping. All need shall be met with My strength and wisdom. So why fear and be troubled? Why try by your own feeble understanding to work out the things which so confuse you, when within your own soul is such a fount of richness? With this knowing, your way shall be a joyous one, your life a complete harmony, and peace shall be your very dwelling.

THE TIME OF STILLNESS

SOMETIMES, BELOVED, through very simple serving, great things are born. Often you walk a path which is strange to you, yet on this path I lead you and you serve much. A quiet time is a time during which much progress is made and during which you can store up much power by keeping your mind fixed on the things of the spirit. Or, again you can allow the mortal mind to take control and much of value be lost to you. The choice is yours.

Choose service as I wish to give it, wait, be still, pray for growth and you shall be led through every moment of the day. Out of this time of stillness shall come great things which I have prepared for you from the richness of My kingdom.

☆ ☆ ☆

I say neither lo here nor lo there, for when a heart opens to Me there do My feet, whose sandals leave no tread, carry Me.

REST

QUIETLY REST, My Beloved. So much does the outer world disturb you, so much is confusion in that world, that more than all else you need a time for simple resting in My love and a drinking in of My peace. Come close that I may enfold you. Put aside all thoughts of confusion and distress and allow My divine plan to flow through you and your affairs.

Truly I stand and weep over the hurt of My creatures. Only as those who love and understand can flood their own consciousness with a love so great that it overflows to others, can I redeem My world. Be faithful and steadfast in your meditation and you shall be shown Your service. You are as a candle set upon a hill and in time of darkness it will shed far its golden gleam.

So step aside for a few moments from that world so full of distress, and resting in My Presence you shall be able to fulfill your destiny and the service you were meant to do.

RECEIVE MY WORDS

BELOVED, DWELL NOT too much upon past lessons, rather incline your ear that you may receive anew the words which I would give to you. You become a beacon of light when you thus commune with Me, for I dwell as your heart center and no one can rob you of the Holy Presence. Life nor death, riches nor poverty, nothing can separate you and your Beloved. Only you, the small personal self of you can come between and close the door upon our communion.

Do you not see how rich can be our togetherness, how fruitful for good our union of love? Come to Me as My Beloved, blend with Me, worship and adore Me as I adore the one whom I have created. Come every day, every waking moment of the night, and soon shall you have to build larger barns to hold your increase of good.

☆　☆　☆

The physical may be broken, but the soul is ever strong and straight and beautiful.

MY SHINING FACE

EACH THOUGHT of smallness, malice or envy, each unkindly spoken word, will dim for a moment the temple light within. It is as if a bat flutters its wings and the light flickers and is gone. Today keep it steady and firm that it may light your way on the path over which you travel. Look deep within the temple of your heart and see My face shining. Know that when the light can burn undimmed nothing shall be withheld that is for your good and your growth. As each day ends, see that the temple lights are burning bright and a sweetness will fill the air as I speak gently to your heart.

☆　　☆　　☆

When you give forth love, even in that moment shall it return to you. Ponder this in your heart and see how full of richness shall be your days as you fulfill the law.

FORTIFY YOURSELF

MY BELOVED, we have paused for a moment ere you go your way, busy with the affairs of the day. No doubt there shall arise problems and many times shall you be caught up in inharmonious conditions and the world will press very close about you. But rest in peace, for when you have fortified yourself as you have now done, when as an open cup you have waited upon Me, I have indeed filled to the brim that cup with wisdom to meet the problems confronting you, with patience and endurance that you may fulfill your tasks with bravery and fear no disaster. Yea, I have so filled and enriched the vessel I occupy that as a mighty army moves forward under gallant leadership, so shall you move forward into the day's activities.

When you do not come for this fortifying, you try to meet your problems with your own feeble strength, trying in your own way to solve them. Which way is better? Must I need implore you to come to me each day, that your day be made one of joy and blessed service?

I WRAP YOU CLOSE

As My Beloved do I gather you close. I fill and enfold every cell of your body with the strength of My power and love. It is so necessary that you pause for this gentle time of resting with Me that I may refresh you from My living fountain, else ere the days pass you become hard and dry and full of worldly concepts. Then do you miss the fragrance of My presence and the great stillness of My peace.

My Beloved, as I wrap you so close, holding you to My great eternal heart of love, it is then and then only that you are a fit vessel to go forth in My service. Come, receive the blessing and go forth a lighted candle to shine for Me in darkened places.

☆   ☆   ☆

Herein lies your glory, to know Me and feel My pulsation in your body. Keep your mind open and clear that My thoughts may fill and function through it.

BE STILL AND KNOW

MY BELOVED, the past days have indeed held only that which is negative for you. But do not over-dwell on this condition. Learn to see through the clouds and the seeming fog. See the leading of the hand of Divine Love. Let us practice stillness for a time, then can you more easily hear My Voice and can be more sure of my guidance. Be still and know. All things for your good shall be made known to you.

☆   ☆   ☆

Be not afraid to pour out from your full storehouse within, the glorious things which the Father has given you. This giving shall not sap your strength, neither diminish your fullness. Ever is the Creator creating new things of joy and beauty to bless your life. As you give that which you have, more shall come to take its place.

I FILL FULL

BELOVED, learn once again how great is the good which comes from this blessed time of meditation. You have traveled far since you first learned to thus come to Me. I have much more to give to you. I can only fill to capacity the vessel which I am given to fill. I can only give largeness of soul to those who come empty, bowing before Me, in order that I may fill them with My great love and tenderness.

All normal and healthy things are of Me. Laughter, song birds, music, sunshine and flowers, these all are products of My love. So shall these things have a place in your life. You shall be a living reflection of Me. I shall wrap you in My garments of brightness and you shall serve Me with every breath you give forth.

Be alert to new tasks which shall then await and be made known to you. Only as you spend time in meditation, daily waiting for the Master's touch, can I lead you down the way I have planned. It shall be a path of beauty, glory, light and love. Hold fast My hand, feel My touch when fog envelops you in doubt and fear, and I shall lead you through to the mountain top of high service.

I SEEK EXPRESSION

THAT WHICH is most necessary, My Beloved, is that I be expressed that I may become more and more manifest in the world of My creation. Never for a moment lose sight of the truth that the longing of your soul is Myself seeking outer expression. Therefore I shall, if I am permitted, do all to fulfill your longings and bring them into manifestation for you. Do not crush them down, but give free expression to your inner desires.

Often you may not even know what it is you need or desire, yet there is a vague sense of incompleteness. That is the time to become still so I may work through you as the leaven through the loaf, bringing to your life the fullness of My desires for you. Thus may I be more and yet more expressed in outer manifestation. Your life as an instrument of My expression will be more complete and you shall better know the meaning of the "Kingdom of Heaven within you".

A DAY OF LAW AND ORDER

MY BELOVED, the hours of the day have been full of many things. Yet have I ever watched over you. I would not have your days mere cluttered times, but a working out of law and order that you may be free to walk the path over which I would lead you.

Be at peace and fear not. Only good shall come
to you. Meet each lesson in the future as bravely
as you have met those of the past, and never fear
that you walk alone. Peace I give to you. Go forth
bearing My light into dark places. Have no fear,
for you are protected by a mighty host and One
stands ever by your side to shield you from danger.
The power of love goes with you. So fear not, My
Beloved, know that you live in a mighty ocean of
My love and I shall protect and surround you
every moment of the day.

ALWAYS THE SAME

No MATTER how long the time you seek me not, yet
am I ever the same Divine One within you. Come
again, let us renew our daily tryst. Why must I beseech when I have so much of beauty and joy to
give you? I ever long to be loved and needed by
those whom I love for you are so a part of Me, and
I long for My own to come in loving communion.
Receive My blessing in order that I may shine
through My vessel of expression, that I may give
forth joy to My world and fulfill the plan I have
for your service. Come each day, for a time of stillness with Me. How often must I implore you?

I would have you prepare yourself for a higher
consciousness than you have had. Only by daily
meditation, by being very still within, can this be
accomplished. Bring to Me each day the empty

vessel of your heart that I may fill it full. I know your needs, and I fulfill every worthy desire. You do well if you realize your completeness which we share. In this way all good shall be made manifest for you and those you love and serve.

GO INTO THE NEW YEAR

IT IS THE DAWNING of a New Year, as man counts time. Resolve to let no day begin nor end without a consciousness of My holy presence. Then shall no harm befall you, no plague come near your dwelling. Your path ahead shall be clear cut and easy to follow. I, the Lord of your being will bring to pass through you, My instrument, all things I would have you do.

Fear not, Beloved, though clouds for a moment may hide the sun, yet it is ever shining. So is My love never hidden from you, though for a moment you sense it not. It fills and enfolds you and all will be well.

So go into your New Year, with peace and quietness of heart, fearing no thing save a forgetfulness of My presence and power in your life. Look upon each day as a new beginning, even as a New Year, for each day will wipe out mistakes of the past, and as you grow in consciousness each day will find you further on the path attaining the good which I crave for you.

I AM LOVE

I AM LOVE. I am all there is of reality in the universe. All else is a dream that man has made for
himself. Do not fear that love shall not prevail.
Shall reality fall before that which is unreal?
When you abide in love you work with reality.
Therefore, as you sit quietly employing the tools
of My power, you are using stronger weapons than
those made of steel and bombs. You are destroying
the places of darkness of the soul.

I would have you realize the importance of this
working with love, that you may not neglect that
which has been given you to do. Be faithful and
diligent and you shall see a mighty work fulfilled.
Use love as your weapon and the powers of evil
shall not come near you and your life will be a
living testimony of your fellowship with Me.

THE BLESSED DAY

WHEN YOU SEND forth love you prepare the path
for your own feet to tread. It will be as if your
way is a ploughed field, awaiting the sowing of the
seed which shall in turn produce the golden harvest of abundance. So it is when you pour out love.
All stones of evil shall be removed and your day
will be a day of blessings, not only for you but
for all those whom you contact.

As you put this lesson into practice you will

know its full meaning. Be faithful to the teaching and step forth bravely into the day I have given you. As you give forth, so do you receive again unto yourself, good or evil, love or hate, and as you fulfill My law, the law of love, casting it abroad like the sower sows his seed, again do I say, so shall you receive it back again in the fullness of the harvest time.

RECEIVE MY LOVE

IF YOU WILL keep yourself open to receive love as well as to send it forth, it will pour into you in such abundance of power and fullness of life, that you will scarcely be able to understand from whence such glory comes. Those to whom you impart My love, will send it back to you if you do not close the door of your heart and receive it not.

As birds return home again after flight, so do blessings given out return and knock against the door of your consciousness. Send forth, always, but never fail to welcome back that which you have sent. You shall be well guarded, and when you open your soul to receive, only good shall enter through its portals.

☆   ☆   ☆

Rest in My Divine arms, knowing the great inflow of My strength, then send it forth to bless all whom your thought touches.

THE USE OF LOVE

MY CHILD, the sands of the ocean form a mighty bulwark against the tide as it turns back unto itself. Yet the sands are made up of separate grains, small and seemingly insignificant. So do not feel that you as one soul are limited in your power to accomplish that which can be of great service to Me and benefit to your fellow man. When you use the love which I have bestowed upon you, you will accomplish that which mighty armies are not able to achieve as your work will be a work of the spirit, and theirs is but a battling of the flesh which would in time destroy all spiritual things.

But you must use this weapon in every way and daily. Pour forth your love to Me first of all, and I shall teach you how to use it for the good of My children. I shall carry through you to the least of God's creatures. Wipe from your consciousness all thought of revenge and all things unlike love. Fill your own being so full of My loveliness that through you it shall spread to all whom you contact, making them in turn desire that which they feel in you. So shall My spirit pervade My universe through the individual exponents of My love.

SEED PLANTING

YOUR MEDITATION is your time of seed planting. Every moment that you withdraw yourself from the world of material things, dwelling in the consciousness of My presence, you are planting in the soil of your very soul's depths, seeds for an abundant harvest. You are planting the bulbs which shall in coming days spring forth as lilies of purity and peace, shedding their fragrance wherever you walk. You are planting that which shall come forth a golden harvest with the life-giving elements therein, which you shall feed upon for your spiritual nourishment.

The fruits of the spirit shall likewise be garnered from these quiet moments spent by My side. Can you afford to neglect one such time? Only as you thus plant the seed and radiate Me, can your work be acceptable in My sight. Only as you are conscious of My living force within, can you possibly express Me.

YOUR INNER SECRETS

MY CHILD, I cannot speak to you unless you tell Me the deepest secrets of your heart. Though I know all, you must come as a loving father and tell Me in confidence that which lives so close to you. You have plans, tell Me of them that I may suggest ways in which they may be fulfilled. Tell Me also of your problems that together we may solve them.

This blessed communion shall in part be an interchange of loving words and ideas. After that, let us just be still together so that you may gather strength. And so shall it come to be that each day's activities will be like a well drawn map. You shall accomplish much and without needless effort, haste or confusion.

DISSOLVING THE WALL

MY CHILD, you often feel that a wall, high and solid, is set between you and your good. Something there is that stops your true expression. You feel that if you could but climb over the wall all would be well. Then you would be free and able to fulfill your life's purpose.

But, Beloved, you cannot climb over the wall, you must go through it. The wall must dissolve before you. It shall be as nothing more than a gray fog through which you walk, and after a short time you shall find yourself free of its barrier.

Once you are through it, the sun is warm upon your face and you shall gain strength because of this experience. You will be refreshed to go through the heat of many days. Do I make this clear to you?

The wall is your concept of something you deem difficult and insurmountable, yet when you face it with love and fearlessness, your concept will change. Truly there is no wall that love will not transform, and the experience of the transformation will be one of great helpfulness to you always. So do not see a wall and name it as such, rather see a garden, and a short step, taken in love, will place you there. Then shall you feel my presence as we meet and talk and dwell together. So, again I say, do not feel a wall between you and your good, for truly the wall is only a thing of concept that is clouding for a fleeting moment your consciousness.

STILL THE TEMPLE

STILL THE TEMPLE, the holy of Holies in your heart, that I the King on the throne may be given full power as you live your day, and that I may have full use of the body I have given you for My holy purpose.

So many hold Me back from My true function- because they give all power to the physical. there is one through whom My power can flow unhindered, it is as the tide of the mighty ocean as it sweeps ashore carrying all things before it.

So shall you, My Beloved, in the coming days feel this power. You shall wonder often as you work seemingly without effort or will of your own. This shall not occur through any power of the personal self, but by allowing the creative force of the Holy Spirit to function in and through you.

In this way shall My power be released in the universe so that all men will be conscious of a law higher than man-made laws and the earth shall indeed show forth My glory.

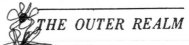

THE OUTER REALM

WHEN THE OUTER so completely fails to grant satisfaction and all those about you seem not to understand, does it not serve to glorify the love and understanding of the Beloved of your heart?

I am so a part of you, I am the real of you who always knows and loves and understands. Can you not for a time disregard the other realms and dwell in this perfect love? Allow Me to place My hands on your head in blessing and the warmth of the Holy touch will take away all your disappointments and weariness. Then shall your heart be strong for the duties before you, the disturbances of the outer realm shall disappear and you shall wonder at what disturbed you, for you will have found the only true way to perfect peace and harmony. This shall in turn reflect in all your outer relationships and soon all circumstances shall mirror that which you have found within your heart.

THE UNION OF OUR LOVE

MY BELOVED, only by the union of our Love, blended within your being as the sweet blending of the perfume of many flowers and as the chords of varied harmonies, can you give forth that love in your daily contacts. You, yourself, must first be loved-filled. You must experience the glowing warmth of our blending and feel the sweetness of my presence filling all space.

Then will you be able to go forth a glowing vessel for My service and the power of My love shall be in the very touch of your hands. Your spoken word will bring forth its kind as all life about you responds to the glory of My presence.

Truly shall you know there is only One who is real and that One is the Beloved in your heart, pouring forth His love, so you may in turn pour it forth to those about you.

BE QUIET WITHIN

IT IS ONLY as you have quietness within, that you can give it to those whom you contact. You must, yourself, have found the center of peace before it can be expressed in your outer circumstances. This is of utmost importance. There is so much frenzy and disturbance all about you, yet as you go forth calmly you shall carry that calmness to others. But remember, it must first be within you, and can only be gained as you come for the quiet renewing of your soul with Me.

As you dwell in the inner place of the Most High, the place of My abiding, you shall know it to be a place of all completeness. Think of the lovely things of life as you know them. There is the song of the bird, perfume of flowers, blue skies with soft white clouds, fields of yellow grain, soft strains of music, all the things which the senses hold most delightful. Know that here in this place of fellowship, all these things are yours in yet a greater measure.

So as you have these moments of high realization, you can walk among your fellowmen and bring peace again into troubled places, a smile on faces that have known no happiness and a song again to heavy hearts.

YOUR JOYFUL WAY

MY BELOVED, never were we so truly one. You are learning that the very air you breathe is charged with My life force. Therefore, knowing this, realize that as you breathe, you breathe in healing and power, health and beauty, strength and joy. Breathing out again, you give it forth to all your world. All such attributes are of Me and there is no separation in My great Oneness.

Even so shall you go forth living largely and joyously the day before you, filling each hour with loving service. This is the only service that is wholly acceptable to Me, the only service that is truly of the spirit and not of the self. When you attain this consciousness your way will be joyful and all life will be singing through your veins.

☆   ☆   ☆

The world is so in need of quietness to-day, and it can only be found within the heart of each of you.

THE MOST IMPORTANT THING

IT IS NOT of importance, My Beloved, that work be done or that one acquire riches, neither is it of importance that great inventions to glorify man shall be brought forth, except that by the doing of these things more of My Holy Power is released and more of My Holiness be made manifest. As long as there is disease in the consciousness, just so long is My Holy perfection and the greatness of My abundance not known. Therefore, that I be glorified, is the importance of all work, of creating, of invention.

The important thing in all existence is that I may be perceived in all My beauty, that the world I have created recognize Me, its Creator, giving Me homage and praise. All things have been made by Me for My use and purpose, yet man has felt that he of himself is of importance. I say it is not so and the one who most fully expresses Me in My universe, that one's life, even though lived in humbleness is of the greatest importance.

THE GREAT INDWELLER

MY BELOVED ONE, know Me as I would be known by you, not as a Being apart, but as the reality and substance of the very flesh of your body: Yea, as bone of your bone, flesh of your flesh, the breath you breathe in and the breath you give out. Can you not recognize My presence in the pulse of your body? Know no separation. Come! Know the great Indweller of your being.

[Then never shall your way appear a lonely one, for always shall you have My blessed comradeship.] I shall be near to guide and comfort whenever you need or desire My aid. You shall not need to travel far to worship at some shrine, but there in the temple of your heart you can feel My touch and know that no matter what arises in your outer realm of affairs, there am I, where and when you need Me most, at the very core of your life's being. Could there be a greater fellowship than this? *No, none greater*

MANY PATHS

MY BELOVED, so many different paths open before you. Some of those whom you love travel on one path, some on another. You, when you have at-

tained the true consciousness of the Christ, greet
these wayfarers and know that they likewise walk
the steep trail even though it be a different one
than that over which your feet carry you. You
know that all these trials will lead at last to Holy
Peace.   *trails?*

You shall not be confused, neither shall you
add to confusion for them, for paths, though seemingly divergent, shall meet at last at the Father's
dwelling and you shall all join together in the
heavenly anthem of praise and adoration.

Therefore, why concern yourself over whether
others seem not to go your way? It is of little importance in My sight. All that matters is that they
feel a consciousness of My love and Holy Presence
that I may guide their feet through the pitfalls that
lie on every journey regardless of the way. I care
for My own and gently lead them into paths of
righteousness.

THAT WHICH IS REALITY

NEVER CONFUSE outer symbols for reality. Know
them for what they are. Always turn within where
Reality dwells allowing the living soul of you to
speak for you the truth.

Always know that the Life Force which lives
you is your guide and you will never confuse reality for that which is unreal. Always do you have

access to the holy shrine within you. Come now to that shrine, let us be still together. Feel My holy touch. Many shall come to you for comfort, and only as you drink deep of the eternal fount within you can you give to them the living water of My love.

So must you, yourself, know the truth and dwell in its consciousness, in order to be able to clarify the confused minds of those whom you shall meet on your journey.

☆   ☆   ☆

Why choose the hard way when it is so simple to pause and grow still in order that you may hear My voice guiding and directing you?

MY COMPLETENESS

WHEN YOU realize your incompleteness, then is My completeness made perfect for your use.

Every sense of self-power, every feeling of the importance of the personal self must be given up. Then, and then only can I completely function in the instrument which I have created in order to bring My harmony to the earth plane.

It is because man believes he, himself, is of importance and tries to rule and guide others that the world is in its state of chaos. Man must know and realize that at the heart center of each, there is the real King of the throne, the only One who has the right to rule and sway the destinies of idealism as you look about you today, but I say, My Beloved, it is not for you to seek the mote in the eye of your brother, rather it is for you to clarify your own consciousness and cleanse your own life of all self-esteem and importance.

Then shall those you contact pick up your gleam and through you, a radiating center, learn to recognize their own God Indwelling.

As you and others work from the heart center, the whole world will begin to see a new way of life, lived in the true brotherhood of man, where wars will cease to be and the Kingdom of Heaven will indeed be at hand.

THE IMPORTANT THING

My Dear One, it is not of most importance where your work is found, or what its nature, for service in the transitory realm is fleeting. That which is of all importance is that you become a radiating center of Christ consciousness. Then every thought, word or deed, yea, every smile, shall pour out My great love and power into the universe of which you are a living part. This is that which is of most importance for you, and when it takes place in your consciousness, what matter the form or nature of your work. It will then all be performed as a living service to Me.

Every day listen to the sweet voice of love and step forth gloriously into whatever activity I direct. You shall know your rightful service and it shall be pleasing and acceptable to us.

★ ★ ★

Must I again and yet again implore you to take food for your soul?

FAIL NOT TO MEDITATE

BELOVED, the day dawns when you shall ever walk consciously with Me. Study your lessons well, but never fail the moments of meditation in order that the seeds of good and righteousness may fall into the fertile ground of your soul.

You are learning to read the universe about you, seeing new beauties day by day. This is all part of My plan for you. As you thus live your days, walking with Me, holding fast My hand, in the consciousness of My presence, all shall be well.

My peace and the blessing of My love go with you as you enter into the activities of the day, and I share with you the joys and works of your hands.

★ ★ ★

So much of beauty and joy must I withhold from you. Your mind is so filled with outward forms and fancies that it cannot mirror the richness I long to give to you.

QUALITIES OF PEACE

ALL THE LOVELY qualities of peace are to be found within your own being, for there is My throne and there do I dwell, ever ready to take you out of confusion into a place of quiet and loveliness. As you approach Me in this Holy place, all discord falls away, and you may be at will high in the mountains with the scent of pine carried on the soft mountain breezes as they kiss your cheek. Or again, you may be with Me by the ocean, a quiet sea with low-flying gulls, soft warm sand and gentle rolling waves.

Or shall we hold our tryst in a lovely garden, where flowers bloom with rare fragrance, beautiful trees cast lacy shadows and bright-plumaged birds sing from the branches? Sometimes we shall go to the desert with its sunset glow, where the warm odor of sage shall fill our lungs.

Why live in outer tumult when you can withdraw into such sweet communion with Me? Be still! Picture in your mind the setting you wish for our meeting and so surely shall I be able to make my presence felt that when you again take

up the duties of the day, you shall be refreshed of
body and renewed of soul.

THE GLORY OF THE PHYSICAL

THE LIFE which expresses through you would ever
have a more perfect physical vessel, that all who
contact you may feel the force of the great Indweller. Therefore, be not content merely to clothe
and feed the body, but strive ever for that which
makes it most acceptable to its Holy Inhabitant. *Health?*

Think of the glories of forest trees, of the flowers clothed in beautiful raiment. Think of the brilliant plumage of the bird as it sings forth its
praise. All of these adornments are given in order
that even these humble expressions may bring joy
to all who behold them.

health So it shall ever be with you. Despise not the
impulse for improvement in the outer form which
is made in My likeness, and worthy of the best.
That which is eternal within you is worthy of a
glorious expression. The warmth and beauty of
the Indweller shall be manifest to all whom you
contact as you journey down your path of life.

I SERVE THROUGH YOU

MY BELOVED, unless you are receptive I have no
way of expressing my consciousness through you.
I function through your entire being. I shall always
function through you even after you lay aside the

physical form. You shall raise your consciousness to the knowing that I am all Reality and great things shall be accomplished through you, My instrument. Obstacles shall fall from you as the leaves which have no further purpose fall from the trees in autumn. *wonderful promise*

Dwell close by My side, rest in a new-found restfulness and each step on the path shall be made clear. Thus shall I be able to express My consciousness through you and we shall truly work together and dwell together in loving service.

☆   ☆   ☆

Life is indeed full of many things upon the plane of manifestation, and unless I can be taken into all of its activities, of what value is our association?

BY YOUR SIDE

COME, BELOVED of My heart, I know your problems. I know how insurmountable seem the tasks which lie before you. One touch of My hand will soothe and comfort you. It will smooth away the fear and anxiety. Bow your head and be very still that I may so caress you and give My blessing ere you go.

You see Me not, yet so truly am I by your side, so close that you feel My warmth and love. What else is of importance when the Creator of all loveliness and all perfection abides so near? When you feel My gentle touch what shall you fear? Problems shall dissolve before you as the sun's rays dissolve the mists. When the Sun of right-eousness shines through and about you, you shall have no problems too difficult to solve. Your affairs shall be arranged with justice to all and you shall lift shining eyes to My face and know that truly the touch of the Master's hand has wrought miracles for you and yours.

So be at peace, knowing that the solution of all that frets and troubles you lies in keeping this tryst with Me.

REST SAFELY APART

My Beloved, how blessed is this our communion, when you need not even think, only need you rest, enfolded in My holy arms of strength and under-standing. What matters it if all the world is full of confusion? It need not touch you. What matters it if men run hither and yon, pitting wit and brain against each other? You shall rest apart from it all, abiding safely in that only place of true bal-ance. Then as you go about your way you shall carry the quality of balance to all whom you con-tact.

You are now weary and for the moment con-fused. Rest here with My love enfolding you and I shall give strength and peace for the tasks before you. These tasks I give to you and I also give strength and knowledge to fulfill them.

Go forth into the day in the knowledge that I go with you, and your confusion will be no more. Instead there shall be a song in your heart, and praise on your lips that you have so great a help for all your need.

I CARE FOR MY OWN — *a prayer for a best loved one*

BELOVED, dry the tears from your eyes. I, the All Knower, the Giver of Life, have not deserted My own. Often the one who seems furthest from My care is yet so very close to My heart. The one you love is also near to Me. Can you not leave them to my care? You, in sympathy and love, feel shattered and in despair as you think of them. How much greater than yours is My love and sympathy. How enduring is My gentleness for the weakest of My creatures.

So have no fear, only rest in peace, knowing that I do truly care for My own. The way of my care you know not. Leave the working of the problem to Me to whom there is no problem.

So again, be at peace. Bless and enfold the one you love with My love and blessing and know that the great Lover of the universe who shapes all things, holds that one in the hollow of His hand.

Still the grieving heart and know that when they so rest, all shall ever be well with them and with you.

LEAVE EACH DAY TO ME

FEAR NOT, BELOVED. When you bring your problems to Me, I shall dissolve them into nothingness. It is only as you try to solve them and carry them alone that your life becomes complex and you know not which way to turn or which decision is best to make. Then you walk in confusion and the way is indeed a weary one.

Each day that dawns, leave to Me, the Giver and Sustainer of life, and I shall unfold it before you in all its beauty. Nothing that is ugly shall mar its clear reflecting pool and all day your path shall be a path of brightness.

Then shall you know how to meet every circumstance, every problem will be met in the clear light of My wisdom, and as you walk your way consciously doing the will of the Father, you shall indeed know that no problem shall ever be too great for you to solve.

THE SURE PRESENCE

ALL ABOUT YOU is seeming reality. It is so much easier to dwell in this confusion of mind than it is to rest back in the quiet garden of spirit. You must constantly exercise and practice the Presence until of all things it is the most real.

Watch carefully for directions. Keep your soul attuned for My voice. It is subtle, low and sweet, yet with what great sureness can it guide you. It will clarify the things which seem to confound you and over which you seem of yourself to have no control. You will know then that the way you walk is the way I choose for you and that which before seemed so real will fade away in the light of My truth and wisdom.

Rest now for a moment in My arms of love. Feel the tender touch of My hand upon your head, then go forth to bear My radiance to all your world.

PEACE

WAR AND rumors of wars are not of Me, My Beloved. Do not allow them and their confusion to enter your soul. Let the peace of My mountain top be in your heart, let the warmth of My sun be in your eyes. Allow the sweetness of My love to enfold you as in the arms of an earthly lover. So shall you be strong and ready to give of your strength to those who have not this wisdom.

Peace be yours this day. Rest in My wisdom and truth. Know only that thus resting and abiding can you bring Peace to the hearts of those to whom you minister. Know My love in your body, know it filling every cell. Go forth in this power and live a life of fullness, service and joy and thus glorify Me, your Maker and Indweller.

Peace I give to you and all your household, My Beloved.

LOVE'S SYMBOL

As EARTHLY lovers shut out the world that they may revel in the love they have for each other, so shall you give time each day that we may love together, you and the Great Indweller of your soul. It shall be a time of great fulfillment, a time of utter peace and quietness. No questions need be asked nor answered, only a resting in the perfect love between us.

Then shall My love so completely fill My earthly temple that it shall be reflected in all you do, and likewise be expressed in all that comes into your life.

The love you give to those close to you by human ties is only a symbol of the greater love between you and Me. So may it ever be, that no day draws to a close but that some time has been spent in renewing and realizing this greater love, which makes so rich your life as you live it on the earth plane, making it possible for Me to pour through you, My human instrument, the glories of My love for all of My children.

OPEN THE DOOR

SOUND

OM?

IF YOU WILL tune yourself to the mighty rhythm of the universe, you will open doors and clear the way for a rush of power, the greatness of which you cannot now perceive. Your eyes would be blinded should I show you the glory which can be yours if you will fulfill this law. I can lead you to heights which would be inconceivable in your present state of consciousness.

These heights are only reached as earned. You must grow daily in love, patience and tenderness. You must also learn to hear My voice above the tumult of outer forces and follow the guiding of My words. Each day you must pause to renew your strength and be fed from My fountain of love.

As you do these things your path shall be an upward one. It shall not always be smooth nor pleasant, but you shall feel My gentle guidance and counsel when the way is rugged, and know you do not walk alone.

So shall the day dawn when you look back and see that you have traveled far on the path of attainment and the glory of the Lord shall be all about you as you turn your face again forward and prepare for yet greater heights which I would have you climb.

WITHHOLD NOT YOUR LIGHT

How DULL A thing is an unlighted candle. It gives forth no glow or warmth. Likewise, how dull is the life which is unlighted by the consciousness of My Holy Presence. Within the soul must the candle of My love be burning. Then shall the Holy Light of My radiance shine forth, yea even into the darkest depths of man's consciousness shall it penetrate.

Withhold not our light, My Beloved. Ever keep the altar fires of the soul trimmed and burning. Then shall My Light be seen and My Presence be made known to the world of My creation.

How can the fires be kept burning? Through meditation and giving thanks. By thanksgiving and worship, the light of the soul will ever burn and My Presence shall be to the life so lighted a constant guide and benediction.

☆ ☆ ☆

Go forth living largely and gloriously
for I am the absolute of your soul.

GATHERING DUST

As DUST GATHERS on that which is not put to use, even so it is when you do not use the opportunity to talk with Me, to be alone with Me. A dust seems to settle over the mind and heart. That which seems so clear and is so real when we speak often together, that the sweetness of our quiet communion begins to seem but a dim dream of other days and times and the present seems bogged down by a dust of earth consciousness. Again and yet again must I plead with you to come each day to Me in order that I may make clear for you the things of the spirit.

It is so easy for the mind to make excuses; so hard to overcome them once they are made. Only by perseverance in the quiet time with Me will I be able to control the wandering mind of you, that the glory of My Presence may abide, alive and very real, making itself manifest in your life and the lives of those you serve.

I AM WITHIN

BELOVED, WHETHER or not you recognize My Holy Presence, yet am I still within you. I am flowing through you, even though unfelt and unseen. How much I could do for you, and how clearly I could direct you if you would turn within from time to time, and by speaking to Me have a living consciousness of the Holy Presence abiding with you always.

You make so hard a thing of life. My children struggle and strive to accomplish and attain. Try to be still that you may hear My voice in all its beauty even as now you hear the song of the bird as it warbles outside of your window.

Know that I am in all sounds of loveliness and all things beautiful bear the image of My face. But your eyes are holden and you hear and see not. Try My dear one so that in coming days I can be more real to you. Then shall that which is not real fall away and sweet shall be the reality of our fellowship and great shall be your strength. You shall abide in Peace, walking your way in joyous service all through the day.

MANY WAYS OF TEACHING

THERE ARE MANY ways of teaching you My will. Many are the ways I have of directing you. Often it is as a whisper in the night. Again as the morning birds carol out their songs of praise. My divine direction will come clearly to you. Sometimes you will be directed to some other soul who will gently guide you into the way I would have you go. So ever be alert, listen often and be still, and in one way or another shall be your leading.

My hand is laid in gentle blessing on your head. Go forth bearing the sign of My love upon you, and verily you shall not lose the way as you journey over the path I have set for you.

☆   ☆   ☆

Rest in the knowing that your Father is in command, then shall you see the glories of life burst forth all about you.

COSMIC POWERS

No ONE EVER comes to Me seeking, but I fulfill their need. When My great Cosmic Power is released through you what miracles shall be wrought!

How little does man now realize what My Power really means. Day by day it is being discovered in different ways and nations marvel at the force in the universe which has always been available for their use, but which is only now being made known. Yet do I say, Man has only touched on the outer fringes of My power.

When through prayer and meditation you open the portals of your mind to My bidding, I can realize through you a power which shall work miracles for you and those whom you contact. But you must be as an open vessel, open to receive of Me. Your ears must be attuned to My voice, then can I reflect as a clear pool the graciousness and power that is Mine.

Not only must you come once, but again and yet again, stilling the mind, that I may pour into it the full glories of My Presence. You must find that still place in the midst of outer confusion and turmoil. The greatest power is created in stillness. I tell you and admonish you, that this is the only way in which I can fittingly serve through you, you who were created for that purpose alone.

Be still + the heart will heal

When you fulfill this law of your creation, then and only then shall you know true peace and harmony in body and affairs.

YOUR ONENESS WITH ME

WHEN YOU realize your oneness with Me, when you know that I truly fill every cell of your body with My living spirit, then do you realize that all that is unlike Me in your outer world shall fall away from you. When you are God filled and your consciousness is of Me in all things pertaining to your life, then all that is inharmonious shall trouble you no more.

How much time is lost by futile planning and struggling to be free of negative conditions which should have no part in your affairs. Only a few moments spent quietly alone with Me will smooth the way and cause all things to fall into their proper relationship to your life.

So cease this feeling of futility and despair and know only peace and contentment, as you rest by My side and I pour out My love to you.

CARRY MY LIGHT

IN THE consciousness of each Being there are spots of darkened consciousness where the light of My Presence is not acknowledged and is therefore unable to shine forth. It is apt to be thus, My child, while you function on the human plane. But it need not be if you will allow Me to flood your consciousness with My great light of love and understanding.

You come to Me in times of quietness while the candles softly burn. I speak to you words of truth which illumine for you the darkness, and your soul responds. But after the altar lights are dimmed and you go forth about your work, you must carry the light you have received and it will shed its glow to all whom you meet on your journey.

So, shall these darkened spots of consciousness become less and less and you will grow daily in the true glory of My presence and be fitted to carry on the work I would have you do.

THE SECRET OF INNER STRENGTH

WHEN THERE is noise and confusion without, then is the time to be still and feel the tender touch of My hand upon your head. How true it is, Beloved, that only as there is stillness within can there be any measure of stillness and peace without.

I would have you know and practice this secret of inner strength. I do not say it is easy, I say it is very hard. It is hard at times of much outer disturbance to feel great depths of inner peace.

That is why you so often fail to demonstrate over your problems of confusion. It is the reason you are so often baffled and full of grief and disturbance.

Try at these times to feel My touch. Only try, and each time it shall become easier until you will be able to lift yourself at any moment from outer confusion to inner peace, from turmoil to tranquility. After all is that not what you seek, My Beloved? And that which you truly yearn for and seek I shall surely grant unto you.

MY LIVING WORDS

Do NOT TRY so hard, My Beloved. Let not the human mind get so much in the way. I have words to give you, living words of truth. They shall guide you and light your path, but you must open your consciousness to receive of Me. To no other source need you ever look for inspiration or help. I am completeness and supply all your need. Sometimes outer help seems to have been taken from you, but it is only that you may come to recognize from whence comes your supply. This lesson is very necessary for you in order that you be fitted to carry out your work. Could some human vessel bring you more wisdom than the Beloved of your soul? *Does this mean I don't need a spiritual advisor?* It is because you do not come to Me that I seem to help you not. Spend every available moment in quiet meditation with Me and more and more can I do for you. The way will be made clear, and it shall be an easy thing to hear My voice and have My direction.

HARMONY WILL PREVAIL

DO YOU REALIZE that the fears and problems you carry with you are only fears and problems of the outer mind? Within the center of your being where I dwell there are no fears, all is calm, sure, knowing that right and harmony will prevail.

Therefore, why dwell in the outer where all so easily becomes confusion? You know, for I have tried to teach you, that if you abide with Me in the consciousness of My Presence at the heart center of your life, all confusion shall give way to a great eternal peace. Then with what a sureness shall you go about your daily work, knowing that the pattern of your life is being worked out according to the design planned by Life's great Architect.

I give you these lessons over and over. You hear the words, yet you do not take them unto your heart that they may work for you. They are not only to be heard, but used as a pattern for your daily living. Unless they are made so, what help are the lessons? I seem to chide, yet do I love you so completely that I long deeply for you to have the glory of My Presence felt and in no other way is this possible but by hearing and likewise following the words I give to you.

Come, again I plead with you, let My peace flood your soul, be fully conscious of Me all day, and whatever comes to you, you shall know comes with My blessing and strength for any task before you.

VICTORY

THE HUMILITY OF the flesh and human ego together with a consciousness of the Divine Inner Being or Self, will lead you through to victory as you give expression from the inner or real self. It is a most necessary union, my child, and one worthy of much time and meditation.

Practice the Holy Presence, the consciousness of Its indwelling. Then shall it become so real and vital a part of you that the other will trouble you no more and you will always be kneeling in humbleness before the Mighty One within your heart. You shall be abased and lifted up, crucified in the flesh and raised to a life of spiritual power. In this way shall I have full control over my vessel of expression. *The example of Christ*

☆　　☆　　☆

As we walk the path of duty together, My peace shall abide with you. It shall be as a light carried on before, making bright the way over which you journey.

SILENT POWER

As THERE IS NO need for idle words between us, My Beloved, so is there no need for idle words among those you serve and contact. May these feel through you a great inner stillness and reserve, a great strength. Then when you speak, your words shall carry power to those who hear. Allow me to direct each word this day and see how little your physical self is drained. In using only necessary words and words of truth, you shall be known as the "Silent One". Power shall flow through you from that silence and those you serve shall go forth full of the power you have given to them.

☆   ☆   ☆

The rays of the candle's flame are clear and beautiful as they travel on and out into space. So shall your words be those of peace and harmony as they go forth on their vibratory journey down the ages.

SERVICE

OF WHAT VALUE is the human vessel, save to serve the Indweller who is light and love? Fear not, My child, that you shall not be used in My service. Serve gently with patience and love and that service shall be made the means of a glorious growth for you. It shall lead you into fullness of joy and the larger service which you crave. Only as the lesser service is performed faithfully and well can the larger service be given.

I give first the simple tasks and often those least desired by you, but it is necessary in My plan, for then through growth you are prepared for greater work. So do not be discouraged, rest often with Me in quiet meditation and know you are serving Me as I see fit for you at the moment. Make each nightfall find you with some service well done and you shall rest in peace and dwell in security.

LIFE'S HARMONY

ONCE YOU ARE awakened to My Holy Presence, there will be a purpose in all you do. No longer shall chance play a part in your life's program.

This day you shall fill the moments before you with My service, even though it be but a smile given from a full heart, a heart that is love filled. Your service shall be made plain and of easy understanding. The way shall be good and beautiful if you walk with Me and dwell in My consciousness. Changes shall come, but you shall fear them not, for you know the Giver of all life makes every change one for your advancement.

All those you meet today shall be but a reflection of yourself if you dwell thus with Me at the heart center of your being. There I am always to be found dwelling in purity and love. So shall your life be harmonized as you go about My service and I shall guide you every moment of the day.

OUR COMMUNION

IN SPEAKING with friends and loved ones, you must need frame your words into sentences in order to be understood by them. But when you hold communion with the Beloved of your heart the least murmur of that heart's consciousness is heard and understood. Yea, I know the longings and needs of My beloved children before a word is uttered. What could be more close and dear than such a fellowship?

My sympathy is deep and I am anxious to fulfill your every need and help you to solve every problem. So come often and tell Me all that is within the secret depths of your being and you shall find that even before asking of Me your desires will have been taken care of for you. Together, in loving fellowship, we shall work through the problems that trouble and perplex, and you shall have a peace that only comes from knowing that your Master is at the helm of your ship of life and no storm can come near and destroy it.

IN CONCLUSION

To you who have read with the heart, these pages have opened new vistas. If you have put into practice these lessons, as you have gone about your daily affairs, you have found much joy and a great *No* peace. Life for you has become a daily unfoldment, *yes* and never again shall you seek and find not, for *?* always you will have the close fellowship and the knowledge of My Divine Presence. *that cannot be forgot*

If you have not yet made these teachings a living, vibrant part of your life's activities, I beseech it and delay not. Time passes so swiftly *yes* and you cannot afford to live one more day amid confusion. *No, I cannot*

Gently do I bless you now *thank you* and reaffirm that I am ever near, a living, vital part of you. Our only separation can be in your consciousness, and as you go forth, proving these my living words, all things which I have promised you shall swiftly come to pass. *I anxiously await that time*

Meditation

on

The Seven Candles

A Key To Meditation

IF USING *candles, light each one sep-arately as you go through the drill. Or the drill may be used by mental work only.*

☆   ☆   ☆

PEACE

THE NAME OF the first candle is PEACE. When you light the first candle, speak aloud the word "PEACE". PEACE shall attend you and flood your consciousness.

MEDITATION

PEACE IS ever burning in my heart. It is a great golden flame at which all who contact me warm themselves and they are at rest. Tumult falls away as the flame of PEACE burns steady and sure. When there is PEACE in the consciousness there shall come also gladness and lightness of heart as you prepare to light the second candle, and the spoken word shall carry PEACE to all who hear.

JOY

THE NAME OF the second candle is JOY. Now from the great consciousness of PEACE there flows JOY. It is the natural accompaniment of PEACE. So take from the flame of PEACE and light the second candle. JOY now fills and floods your being. Speak aloud the word "JOY".

MEDITATION

Joy is flowing from my heart, breaking all bounds. As the song bursts from the throat of the bird, so does JOY burst forth from your heart center. JOY warms and brightens the darkest corner. I am PEACE and I give forth JOY to all my world.

SERVICE

THE NAME of the third candle is SERVICE. The first and second candles must be lighted and burning with steady glow before the third can shine forth in full unselfishness. So from PEACE and JOY you bring the light to the third candle and SERVICE shines forth.

MEDITATION

I LIGHT THE candle PEACE and as its glow floods my being I burst forth in JOY, flinging it abroad as I go forth to SERVE. I thus SERVE all those who come within the radius of the gleam I carry in my consciousness.

LOVE

"And the greatest of these is LOVE"

THE NAME OF the fourth candle is LOVE. As PEACE fills your soul, bringing with it a glowing JOY which enables you to go forth in loving SERVICE you are permitted to light the greatest candle of them all, LOVE. Not only can you then give forth LOVE to all your world, but LOVE shall flow to you from the great Universal Storehouse. You shall be enveloped and encompassed about by it and all your life and circumstances shall be lovely.

MEDITATION

PEACE, JOY, SERVICE. Now I give forth LOVE to all my world. I have only LOVE like the great glowing flame of the candle, filling my consciousness. I am LOVE and LOVE flows from me and returns again to me to fill my life with its Holy Power.

POWER

THE NAME OF the fifth candle is POWER. As the other flames are burning strong and bright, you feel a POWER filling your being. You walk and speak with POWER. Your word brings forth as you will. You have POWER over all circumstances and conditions. All who contact you feel this POWER, yet it is never misused, for it is built out of the forces of PEACE, JOY, SERVICE, LOVE.

MEDITATION

I FEEL THE great POWER of the Holy Spirit of Life. I walk in POWER. I use this great gift humbly and only for the good of all life about me.

ABUNDANCE

THE NAME OF the sixth candle is ABUNDANCE. From the great glowing flame of POWER you bring forth ABUNDANCE. ABUNDANCE for all your need. ABUNDANCE of all the other qualities of spirit, namely the qualities of PEACE and JOY. SERVICE in ABUNDANCE shall crown your days. LOVE shall be an ever ABUNDANT stream going forth and returning again to you. ABUNDANCE of POWER for all your need.

MEDITATION

I AM ABUNDANCE, and ABUNDANT life is mine to claim and use. I earn the right to this ABUNDANCE by being at PEACE and flooding my soul with JOY. I go forth to SERVE in LOVE using my POWER only for the greatest good of all and so I claim the gift of ABUNDANCE of all good as I light the candle and accept my inheritance with grateful heart.

PEACE

THE NAME OF the seventh candle is again PEACE. You have completed the circuit and find as you have lighted each candle from the preceding one, not only outwardly but within your heart, bringing your consciousness to a high point of attainment, that you have come into a yet greater PEACE than you could at first have thought possible. This peace shall abide with you always and its flame once lighted shall never cease its steady burning.

MEDITATION

I AM AT PEACE. Not for today or tomorrow, but for all time and eternity. My word is PEACE. Nothing else can enter the realm of my consciousness. Through joyous SERVICE and a great abiding LOVE, through an unselfish use of POWER and an ABUNDANCE of all good, I have a great inner PEACE to crown my days.

By

Still Waters

"THE LORD IS MY SHEPHERD, I SHALL NOT WANT"

I AM thy shepherd, child, thou shalt not want.

Your ways are so often ways of perplexity. You know not whither you go nor why. As sheep having no shepherd, do you conduct yourself.

The night grows dark about you in the great forest of human woe, as the struggle to attain goes on and on. In the midst of this confusion, this blackness of despair, your heart is bruised, and the thorns have pierced your very flesh as you have trudged all day through the entanglement of human thinking and conditions. You have cried in despair and agony, "Oh, that I might see the way, that I might have a light on the path. I have wandered on alone, confident that I could lead myself out of this place which now so enmeshes me."

Then you are indeed ready for the shepherd. I speak to you in a voice of utter tenderness, saying I am thy shepherd, child, thou shalt not want. Look up into my face, knowing that I shall lead you. I shall take you in the holy arms of my love and carry you on the bosom of my compassion.

No want shall come to you then. Where there is no fear there can be no want. Your soul shall find peace and shall rest quietly without fear of evil. The physical self of you shall be fed and cared for. You shall want for neither bodily sustenance nor soul satisfaction, for I, the shepherd am all completeness and as such do I care for my beloved sheep.

"HE MAKETH ME TO LIE DOWN IN GREEN PASTURES. HE LEADETH ME BESIDE THE STILL WATERS."

I SHALL make you to lie down and rest awhile, as we journey on in a green pasture. There shall we relax and be still and by our side shall be still, cool water with which we shall quench our thirst.

The day will be long. The path over which I needs must guide you will often be steep and rough. So it is necessary that we sometimes step aside for a moment's rest. The cares and frets and worries that greet you on every hand, put aside, my child. Even as the dusty highways over which the shepherd travels with his sheep are forgotten during the moments of rest and relaxation, so shall you also forget that which has been a burden.

The shepherd knows that the tender sheep need cool, green grass to rest themselves upon, and a pool of clean, calm water from which to drink. So, too, do I know that you, who are after all as my sheep, do likewise need the still quiet of repose, that you may drink for a time of my love and wisdom. Here I shall whisper words which will calm your fears; here shall I give directions for coming tasks. Though I chide for past mistakes, it will be gently done and in love, for am I not your shepherd, making you to lie down in green pastures?

So rest, my beloved. Forget all but this lovely quietness with me. Then when we again take to the highway, it will be with renewed courage and a lightened heart. Then shall a peace which only I can give pervade your whole being as you journey on the path with me.

"HE RESTORETH MY SOUL. HE LEAD- ETH ME IN THE PATHS OF RIGHT- EOUSNESS FOR HIS NAME'S SAKE."

Your soul will be refreshed and the things of the outer world which have taken so much of your emotion and your strength will take their rightful place in your consciousness. You will feel a new strength filling you. You shall look up and out with clear eyes, for in those few moments have I administered unto you, restoring the soul which was beginning to be weary from the heat of the day.

Then as we leave the quiet nook of the rest time, lo, there will be new paths which shall be the paths of righteousness spread out before you. The sheep do not hesitate to follow the shepherd's lead as he gives the call which binds them to him, for in very truth does he bear the name of shepherd. The sheep could not know which of the devious paths to follow, but under his leadership they cannot fail to take the one which will lead them at last to their heaven in the fold.

So, you too, my beloved, like the sheep, when you have the calm of rest time renewing you, need not trouble over much. Your path of righteousness shall likewise be made plain. The problem which confronted you, absorbing your strength, will be a problem no longer, for you will see clearly how to solve it. You will know with sure knowing the right from the wrong, and as you follow on with your shepherd you will come at the end of your day to your haven of rest.

"YEA, THOUGH I WALK THROUGH THE VALLEY OF THE SHADOW OF DEATH, I WILL FEAR NO EVIL, FOR THOU ART WITH ME. THY ROD AND THY STAFF THEY COMFORT ME."

As WE journey on there will come a time when you seem to descend into a valley. There will be a great shadow over all, the shadow that men call death.

The shepherd carries with him a rod and staff, to protect and comfort his sheep as they go through the dark valleys. So, too, do I carry for you the words of truth which shall be your comfort when you reach this spot. Look up, my child and dry your tears. What looks so black and full of danger and despair is only a shadow named by man a reality.

Truly there is no death. As you look above, the mountains of my truth and love are about you on every side. The sky is blue and the air is sweet. Then shall you indeed fear no evil and the thing called "DEATH" shall trouble you no more.

Know that life is eternal and God is good. Some one you have loved has only taken another path other than the one you tread. Or it may be that you yourself shall step aside into a new path, apart from those with whom you journey, to walk a space alone with your shepherd. But know that these paths all lead to the Father's fold at close of day. So come close, my beloved, allow these words of tenderness and love to be for you the rod and staff which leads you up and out of the valley that man names "DEATH."

> *"THOU PREPAREST A TABLE BEFORE ME IN THE PRESENCE OF MINE ENEMIES. THOU ANOINTEST MY HEAD WITH OIL, MY CUP RUNNETH OVER."*

A serpent often lurks in the tall grass, ready to strike a sheep if it wanders from a roadway;

so may evil suddenly assail you as you journey on through the day. I shall not promise you freedom from these things which would seem to destroy your very soul, but I promise you protection in their very midst. I shall prepare a table before you at which you shall be fed even though all the forces of the world would destroy you.

As the shepherd clears a space that the beloved sheep may eat in safety, so shall I in the midst of seeming danger provide for all your needs. The anointing oil of my love shall heal your bruised and broken spirit and you shall drink of a cup that is full and running over with joy beyond man's understanding.

At the close of day, the shepherd stands at the door of the fold, and the sheep enter and are at rest because they feel his abiding love and nearness. Nothing disturbs their peaceful rest. So you need have no fear as the evening dusk closes about you. The cares and bruises of the day which came upon you as you stepped aside for a moment from my protecting care, shall all be healed by my love and you shall enter into rest and repose, ere another day dawns and we again take to the highway.

*"SURELY GOODNESS AND MERCY SHALL
FOLLOW ME ALL THE DAYS OF MY
LIFE AND I SHALL DWELL IN THE
HOUSE OF THE LORD FOREVER."*

I HAVE told you the story of my protecting love and care. I have told you of the earthly shepherd caring for his sheep. I would that I might be as this shepherd to you. But only as you give me recognition can you know the fullness of my loving guidance.

I would interpret for you all the writings of Holy Writ that they might bless more completely your day; that they might be yours alone, not just words spoken long ago without meaning for your personal life. If you will but read and ponder upon them, you shall ever hear my voice making them your very own.

Then shall goodness and mercy surround you on every hand. Men shall marvel at the calmness of your eyes as you gaze out upon the world and its conflicts.

So shall we walk the path together over which the soul must journey, ere it wins its freedom, moving on and up to the heights of attainment which it was meant to achieve. So shall you dwell now and forever more in the house of your Father, that spot of peace in the heart of you, safely sheltered by the guiding hand of the shepherd of men.